AUSTRALIA

Troll Associates

AUSTRALIA

by Laurence Santrey

Illustrated by Allan Eitzen

Troll Associates

Library of Congress Cataloging in Publication Data

Santrey, Laurence.
Australia.

Summary: Describes the world's largest island, which is also the smallest continent and the only continent that is also a single country.
1. Australia—Description and travel—Juvenile literature. [1. Australia] I. Eitzen, Allan, ill.
II. Title.
DU97.S26 1984 994 84-2636
ISBN 0-8167-0124-5 (lib. bdg.)
ISBN 0-8167-0125-3 (pbk.)

Printed in the United States of America

10 9 8 7 6 5 4 3 2 1

Sometime in our planet's distant past, the continent of Australia was connected to Asia by a bridge of land. Then, for reasons nobody can explain, that connecting strip of land was covered by water. And Australia became an island continent, surrounded by the Pacific and Indian Oceans.

Because Australia was separated from the other continents, its animals and plants developed independently from those everywhere else in the world. Today, nowhere else on Earth are there creatures anything like the kangaroo; but Australia has forty different kinds of these hopping, long-tailed marsupials—or pouched animals. They range in size from the rat kangaroo, which is just a foot long, to the red kangaroo, which is the size of an adult human being.

In Australia, there are also strange creatures like the teddy-bearlike koala, the kookaburra bird with its loud rasping laugh, or the world's most unusual mammals—the duckbill platypus and the spiny anteater. The platypus and the anteater are the only mammals that lay eggs.

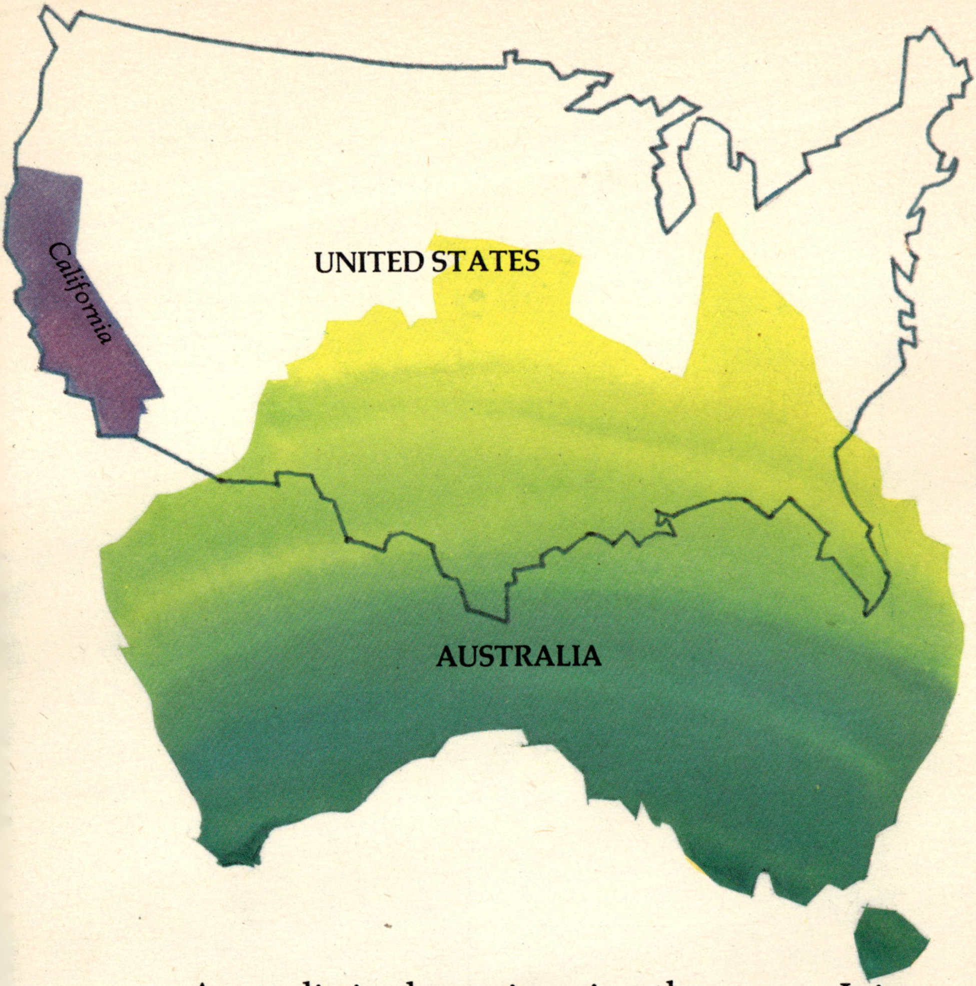

Australia is also unique in other ways. It is the world's largest island, the world's smallest continent, and the only continent that is also a single country. Although its total land surface is about the size of the United States, not counting Alaska and Hawaii, Australia has fewer people than the state of California.

Most of Australia's small population lives along the coastlines, and more than half of those people are in cities. Much of the huge inland area is not very desirable land. Almost half of the interior is desert land. In fact, only the Sahara Desert, in Africa, is larger than the dry, bare, rocky Australian desert.

The Australian interior is so dry that its largest lake, Lake Eyre, often has no water at all. Located in the central lowlands, Lake Eyre was once part of an ancient sea that dried up long ago. Now it has water only after especially heavy rains, and these are rare events. Most of the time, the lake is just a salty bed of mud.

By contrast, the north and east coasts of Australia have enough rain to keep these areas green and lush. And with the continent's moderate climate, these are delightful places to live. Even during the Australian winter, which comes in July and August, the weather is warm enough for people to engage in outdoor sports.

Sports are an important part of Australian life—both in winter and in summer. Tennis, surfboating, swimming, running, cricket, and other sports are highly popular activities. Children start playing organized sports in grade school and often continue as adults.

Australians enjoy a high standard of living. More than half of the population own their own homes. And these are generally modern houses, complete with the latest appliances and conveniences, such as television and radio sets and stereo systems. The automobile is also an important part of an Australian's life, and there are many miles of modern highways, particularly in the coastal areas.

Australia has kept many traces of its British heritage. But mostly its modern cities, its cattle and sheep ranches, its department stores and supermarkets, and its relaxed style of living make it seem like the American West. As in the American West, there is a feeling of wide-open spaces and unlimited freedom of movement.

Australians also have a strong sense of individualism. Much of the outback, which is what Australians call the thinly settled interior, is used for cattle ranching. Most Australian cattle ranches, called stations, are enormous. The largest Australian station is larger than the state of Connecticut. With stations so large, a rancher's neighbor may be hundreds of miles away.

When outback children are ready to start their education, they are sent off to live at schools in the cities, or they learn from the "school of the air." The school of the air is a two-way radio system that links the children with teachers who are many miles away.

In Australia, two-way radio is used for many purposes. Since there are many areas without telephone lines, people talk to faraway friends by radio, and they call for medical and dental services by radio. When they do, the Royal Flying Doctor Service sends in a doctor or dentist by small plane. In fact, travel by small plane in the outback is nearly as common as car travel is in the cities.

The city of Sydney was first colonized about the same time as the American Revolution. The British had been shipping their convicts to America, but when war broke out there, they could no longer do so. They began sending their convicts to Australia instead.

Of course, not all of those who settled in Sydney were criminals. Many of them were people who could not pay their debts, and many others were religious or political protestors. In those days, people were sent to prison for such offenses.

But Britain's prisons were crowded. So the convicts were shipped out of the country to a penal colony where they were put to work for the length of their sentence.

These penal colonies, and the free colonies that were established in the nineteenth century, formed the core of Australia's population. They were hardy, tough people taking on a raw, untamed continent. And even today, although Australia is a very modern place, the character of its people is unchanged. Australians are hard-working, hard-playing, rugged individualists.

When the English settlers reached Australia, they found people living along the coast. These native Australians, called Aborigines, probably arrived when the continent was still attached to Asia. Like their ancestors, they were nomads who wandered from hunting ground to hunting ground. And, like the North American Indians, the Aborigines lived in tribes, practiced sacred ceremonies, and used simple, primitive tools.

Today, some Aborigines live on land set aside for them on reservations. Other Aborigines are farmers and ranchers, and still others live and work in the cities.

Tribal Aborigines, who live on the reserves, are supported by the government. But they are not allowed to vote. Those who do not live on the reserves are treated the same as any other Australian, with all the rights and responsibilities that come with citizenship.

Another group of Australians, the new immigrants, arrived since the middle of the twentieth century. Some, as in the past, have emigrated from Great Britain. Others have come from Southern Europe, North America, and Asia. Australia welcomes these newcomers because the country still needs people to work in its growing economy.

Australia exports millions of bushels of wheat every year. It is also one of the world's leaders in the production of fruits, vegetables, sugar, and dairy products. Its cattle and sheep stations ship meat in enormous quantities all over the world. And one third of all the wool produced in the world each year comes from Australian sheep.

The island continent is also rich in natural resources. More lead is mined in Australia than anywhere else. And the land yields large amounts of coal, iron, opals, gold, copper, zinc, and silver.

Australia has had to import most of the oil it uses. But oil deposits have been discovered that may enable the country to meet its own oil needs in the future.

Industry is expanding at an amazing rate in Australia. This industrial boom began in the middle of the twentieth century. Until then, Australia exported raw materials, such as farm products and minerals, but had to import manufactured goods from other countries.

Today, Australian factories turn out heavy machinery and home appliances, chemicals, clothing, plastics, toys, cosmetics, and just about everything else the country needs. Its auto industry alone supplies cars for the entire Australian market as well as thousands more for foreign countries. Not surprisingly, one out of every three adult Australians is employed by industry.

For all the growth Australia has already experienced, there is plenty of room for more expansion. The outback is still almost empty of people. Of course, much of it has not been fit to live on. But as the land is improved by irrigation, and electric power becomes available to these open areas, all that will change. And as it does, not only Australia but the entire world will profit from it.